Content Marketing:
Get Paid to Repurpose Your Content & Build a Massive Following

by Ben Gothard,
Founder & CEO of Gothard Enterprises LLC
Author of CEO at 20: A Little Book for Big Dreams

The Big Picture

You want to build a following? Great! I want to give you the tools that you need in order to build one based on my experience as an entrepreneur, CEO & author over the past two years. To give you an overview of the process, I am going to teach you how to understand your purpose for building a community in the first place, take that knowledge and figure out exactly who will benefit from being a part of your community, then give you a step-by-step process for maximizing the amount of value that you can provide to that community and using all of that content in order to steadily grow a following over time!

Understanding Your Purpose

Before you set out to build a large following, list, or community of people, you need to understand who it is you are trying to influence in the first place. In business it has historically been called a "target market," but in order modern world we need to think less of firing at targets and more of creating a community of real people. Those that follow you and allow themselves to be influenced by you are those who trust you enough to be a part of your community, and the most effective way to build that trust is to consistently provide them with value.

As an Internet marketer, I believe in using various mediums to distribute content to people that will benefit them and give them value. In this book, I want to share fundamental content production and distribution techniques that I use to grow my following through Social Media, podcasts, writing, and blogging. I have used these fundamental skills and processes to garner tens of thousands of followers in various forms, and that number continues to grow every single day.

How are you supposed to build something valuable if you don't know who you are building it for? The first, and probably most important, piece of the puzzle is understanding who you want to provide value to. You are essentially asking yourself, "who is my community?" However, in order to identify who you are going to help, you need to determine your purpose, your why, for building this community in the first place. Are you trying to solve a problem? Sell a product? Stand for a cause?

As the great Simon Sinek, author and speaker, says, "people don't buy what you do, they buy why you do it." When building a following or a list, you are essentially asking people to buy into your purpose. If you don't have a strong enough purpose to rally people to your side, then you will have an infinitely harder time building any sort of meaningful community. For example, are you trying to help people achieve financial freedom? Do you want to end world hunger? These are powerful purposes that give people a *reason* to associate themselves with you. Once you've identified your purpose, your why, and committed yourself to achieving that thing, write it down here:

_____

_____

_____

Understanding Your Community

Now that you have a purpose to stand behind, you can start to truly understand who it is that you want standing with you. It is not reasonable to think that every single person on the face of the planet is going to want to stand behind you immediately, nor is it an effective use of your time to try and appeal to everybody at once. The most effective community-builders are those who have an "ideal customer." For example, if your purpose is to help other people achieve financial freedom, then your perfect community members could be recent college graduates who are just starting to find their way in the world or stay-at-home moms who want to use some of their free time to make some additional income. Regardless of what your why is, you need to understand your who. By focusing in on your ideal who, you are able to cater to and attract people who share those qualities in an effort to build the community as a whole.

While there are an infinite number of factors to identify an individual, I want to focus on two major areas that are particularly useful to building communities: demographics and psychographics. At the most basic level, demographics include age, location, gender, income level, education level, marital status, and occupation while psychographics involve personality, attitudes, values, interests, hobbies, lifestyles, and behavior, respectively. Now, at first it is going to be extremely difficult to fill in all of these blanks, so start with what you know and improve over time. Once you start actually building your community, you will probably find that some of your initial assumptions weren't 100% accurate anyways. However, the more time you spend understanding your community, the better you can suit their needs and provide value to them.

By diving deep into the persona of your ideal customer, you give yourself two enormous advantages in this process. The first is the ability to identify new opportunities. When analyzing the ideal demographic and psychographic of your specific community, you can and most likely will uncover completely new audiences that you didn't even know would benefit from being a part of your community! The second is the opportunity to position yourself as a unique influencer in your niche. Once you have identified a group of people who need exactly what you can offer, then you can master that niche, add those people to your community, and continue building your following! Over time, you will expand your repertoire, but in the beginning it is crucial that other people see you as someone with knowledge and expertise that they need. If they don't need what you have, they won't give you the time of day, so don't invest your time in any group of people unless you can give them exactly what they need.

Once you've identified your community, your who, and committed yourself to serving these people, write down the persona of your ideal community member here:

_____

_____

_____

Grow Your Community With Content

At this point, you know why you are building a community in the first place and who you are building it for. All that's left to do is actually build it! Before I reveal my personal content creation system, it's important to understand that this process takes time. Just because you spend a day making content doesn't mean anybody is going to care. That's the reality. The people that build real followings do so over an extended period of time by giving as much value as they possibly can to as many people as they are able to reach. Just because you don't gather a massive following in the first month doesn't mean that you are a failure. It takes time to get traction in anything you are going to do, so stay the course, keep providing value to people, and the following will come.

That being said, you should be maximizing every single movement that you make. To clarify, I mean that you need to be constantly producing new content while at the same time repurposing old content and mixing, mashing, and combining everything together into a consistent flow of quality, valuable content for your community. Here's how you do it.

Video: I always try to start off by addressing each individual topic I want to with a video. The reason is that I want to leverage my time most effectively while building a very strong relationship with my community. I typically like to have the camera on me while I'm introducing a topic and then either share my computer screen if it's a technical topic or keep it on me while I explain. Using this process, I find that I can capture the attention of my audience by just being myself and letting my personality shine through. Then, I take the video and put it on YouTube. YouTube is a phenomenal resource for building your following because it is solely focused on video, and, like I mentioned earlier, a video is a lot more conducive medium to build a relationship with another person than any other.

The biggest issue I find with YouTube is that it is hard to get your video seen by a massive amount of people unless you do some keyword research, which most people don't understand how to do. By keyword research, I mean picking the title of your video as well as the tags or search terms that you put in the backend of each video. These are words or phrases that people would search on YouTube in order to find your video. Therefore, you want to find the most relevant keywords that directly relate to your video.

Let's say that you are trying to find keywords for a video about a yoga mat. Go to the YouTube search bar and start typing in a few letters of the main keyword, yoga mat. Type in 'yo,' now stop. Look at the dropdown menu, the YouTube suggested searches, of what you've typed in. These keywords are what everyone is searching for on YouTube. These are the most powerful keywords that relates to these letters. Now type in 'g' and type in 'a' and type in a space. Look at all these results! This is how the keyword system works. This is one of the main ways that I do it.

But there's more. Type in yoga mat and press enter. Now, for this main keyword, you can see all of the top contenders and you can investigate them to see what's working. What keywords are they using? What is their title? You can put your binoculars on, look at their listings, and see what you can replicate/improve on. This is the system that everyone uses, but some people try to overcomplicate it. Picking keywords is as simple as the steps I just mentioned. Practice it, put a smile on your face, and don't look too far into it!

If you really can't think of related keywords or the YouTube suggested search terms are limited, you can head over to Google Keyword Planner. This tool will tell you how many searches per month different keywords receive on Google (and by extension YouTube). This is a quick and easy way to verify your keywords to make sure people are searching for them. Just make sure that you can differentiate your video from the other videos associated with those keywords that you choose!

Audio: Once you start making headway into your video journey, audio is a very logical next step. While you can't make the same connection with individuals with audio as you can with video, there are tons of people who prefer listening to their content while they are driving in the car or working on other mundane tasks. For these people, straight audio is perfect! They can put in headphones and go about their task. The beauty of starting with a video is that you can simply snip your audio from each video and voila, another form of content! Now, make sure you snip the content that is useful without video, like interviews or other audio-heavy content.

I like to take my audio content and upload it for free to Soundcloud.com first in order to get some free exposure. While Soundcloud is predominantly music uploads at this time, it is a great place to put your audio files online for free. Similarly to YouTube keywords, Soundcloud has different "tags" that are used to rank different audio files in the website's native search engine. By doing a little bit of research, you can find the right tags for your audio files to help them get the most free exposure possible.

Once you've optimized your Soundcloud listing, the next step is to take your Soundcloud feed and upload it to iTunes as a podcast. Not only does iTunes give you another free medium to publish your content, but it also helps you reach a massive audience! While typical podcasts are run on a schedule, you don't necessarily have to follow these conventional rules. Whenever you have new content, post it! It's as simple as that, and these new mediums will help you gather even more of a following on various platforms.

Text: Once you've turned your videos into audio, it's time to repurpose again! This time, however, it is going to be text based, and, what's even more exciting is that you can directly monetize your content. All you have to do is transcribe (write down) the audio that you just snipped from your video and edit it into an ebook. By publishing your textual content in the form of an ebook on Kindle Direct Publishing, you can actually get paid to promote your content and grow your following. Not only that, but by utilizing this service from Amazon, you can become a legitimately published author and give yourself more credibility by repurposing the content that you've already created.

If that's not incentive enough, you can also publish your book in multiple formats, giving you multiple streams of income and additional platforms to build your following. With very little effort you can publish your ebook on Amazon's Kindle Direct Publishing. Then, head on over to CreateSpace.com (also owned by Amazon), and turn your ebook into a paperback book. Once the CreateSpace team approves your work, you will be able to get a physical copy of your book and unlock additional channels to sell your work through CreateSpace. The final format is an audiobook (which you've already prepared in the audio step), and by utilizing ACX (once again owned by Amazon), you can simply upload the audio version of your content to another platform. The advantage of repurposing this same piece of content so many times is that you are able to reach a much larger audience. The people who read ebooks probably won't read the paperback version, and the remaining folks will take a listen to the audiobook. All of this is an easy way to monetize all of the content creation that you are doing anyways in building your following while also helping you to reach more people by leveraging Amazon's massive community.

On every single one of these platforms, you will be able to sell through Amazon through one single product page. This makes it easy to funnel all of your Amazon traffic into one place, and gives buyers many options when they are deciding whether or not they want to purchase your product. When ranking on Amazon, utilize the exact same system that you used to rank on YouTube. Keywords are keywords are keywords. The same tactics that work on YouTube will work on Amazon, but the actual keywords that you use may be different. For example, while on YouTube it might be beneficial to include "yoga for beginners" as one of your tags, Amazon might prefer "beginner yoga." You have the tools to do the research, it is just up to you to spend the time making sure everything is optimized.

But, we aren't done yet. Now, since you have video, audio, and text content ready to go, you have the perfect library of content to run a blog! With video you were mainly grabbing traffic from YouTube, now you can upload the videos to your blog. With audio you were mainly leveraging Soundcloud and iTunes, now you can upload the audio straight to your blog. With text you were making your mark on Amazon, so just chop up your books into individual blog posts! Now it's time to put all of these three types of content together to grab some of Google's traffic. One of the most important thing to consider when attempting to rank your website's content on Google is the metadata, including the title of your content and the SEO tags. Getting visibility on Google is similar to ranking on YouTube and Amazon - keyword research. If you spend the time to make sure every piece of content you produce and publish online is fully optimized, you can repurpose everything to become a dominant force in your niche and attract a massive following to you.

Manage Your Community Through Email or Social Media

Now that you're pumping out all of this content, you have to share it and make people take notice. The easiest and most direct way that I've found to do this is through Social Media - namely Facebook, Instagram & Twitter.

Facebook: Depending on what type of following you are trying to build, you should consider either a Facebook page or group. Facebook pages are typically more used for businesses, while groups are useful for more personal endeavors. These two options are very similar, however, and the biggest difference is the ability to use paid advertising on a page. You can invest advertising dollars into a page, but you can't spend on a group.

Regardless of which avenue you take, pick one and stick with it. Using all of the different mediums discussed above, always put a link to your Facebook page or group at the end of your content and encourage people to join for more information or for full disclosure or whatever lead magnet that you choose to utilize. The idea is to funnel all of the free traffic that you're getting from the distribution mediums into one place where you can connect with people on an individual basis. Facebook is a great option because you can chat with people 1 on 1, tag specific individuals in posts that pertain directly to them, and share posts from their Facebook profile to highlight them. Like every part of this process, growing a Facebook page or group will take time. You will need multiple pieces of content pointing people to Facebook for a sustained period of time before your numbers will start adding up to a substantial number.

The good news is that you already have content to keep them there once they do show up. All of your video, image, audio, and text content that you've been creating is perfect content to share with your Facebook community! If these people liked what you were saying enough to opt-in to your community, then giving them more value on the same topic can only make things better. By giving them the content that will continue to benefit them, you are encouraging your community to stay and building trust with your following.

Once you have a sizeable community of people who are active on your page or in your group, you can take the growth a step further by asking them to add some of their friends to the community who would benefit from what the page or group offers. Let's say, for example, that you have 1,000 people in your Facebook group and you've been talking with most of them and building real relationships. You can then ask each person to add 5 people to the group who would benefit from being a part of the community. In one fell swoop, you can go from 1,000 to 5,000 members!

Instagram: Instagram is a fantastic place to share your content in the form of images and shorter video clips. While it is harder to manage a community from Instagram, you can still private message people and build those relationships. As you grow, it will be harder to keep up with everyone, but in the beginning talking to individuals is CRITICAL to your growth and continued success. If your community feels neglected by you, they will leave or become unengaged.

The power of Instagram is that you don't necessarily have to funnel people to this medium. By leveraging smart hash tag use, you can generate an organic following on Instagram and send that traffic to the platform where you are managing your community. Hash tag research is very similar to the keyword research on YouTube, Amazon and Google. You are going to want to start typing in potential hash tags in the Instagram search bar and look at the automatic suggestions. Jot down the top 20 that are relevant to your content, and consistently post with those hash tags included! Here's the trick to it though, you want to strategically pick your hash tags. Just because #art applies to your post doesn't mean that including it will do you any good. In the beginning that hash tag is way too saturated for you to break through. As a general rule, I would pick 10 hash tags with less than 10,000 posts. You need to be the big fish in a small pond in a few different ponds before you can jump into the bigger pond. The next 5 can be hash tags with 10,001 – 50,000 posts, and the final 5 are your heavy hitters with 50,001+ posts. With enough high-quality content and smart hash tag use, you will start gaining some traction and building your Instagram following.

Twitter: Twitter is one of the easiest platforms to build your following simply by sharing content. Think of Twitter like a news ticker on ESPN or the news. It is a constant bombardment of information. How do you get noticed on this platform? Out post your competition! That's right! On Twitter, you can post all of your content in any form you have as much as possible, and it is all right. In fact, tweeting 20+ times a day is one of the few surefire ways to quickly build your following on Twitter.

Like Instagram, you need to strategically pick your hash tags. However, unlike Instagram, you should only pick 5 – 6 main hash tags to hit every single time, and the more traffic these hash tags get the better. You don't want to be posting content with hash tags that nobody sees on Twitter. Instead, you need to jump right into the fray and give more value than anybody else to a few key hash tags. Over time, you will start to get some traction on these hash tags and build up your following. The key is consistency! Once you start getting a steady inflow of followers, you might want to consider funneling them to where you are managing your community.

Putting It All Together

I've shared with you exactly how I create and distribute content to grow my following. The last piece of this puzzle is putting it all together, but I can't do that for you. If you truly want to build a following, you have to put forth the effort to do it. Nobody is going to do it for you, and it is a lot of hard work. There will be a lot of late nights where you are pumping out content and thinking if it is worth it to continue building your following or not. You will have doubts and struggles and problems that you've never dealt with. The good news is that you CAN do it. You absolutely, without a doubt can achieve everything that you are setting out to achieve. Regardless if you want a following of 20,000 or 20,000,000, you can do it. Just know that it will take a lot of work and there are no shortcuts. Those that put in the effort are rewarded. Those that don't are not. It is up to you to make the choice for yourself.

I will leave you with three suggestions to help you on your journey to building an immense following. The first is to set a schedule. With all of this content that you are going to be producing, it will help to have time set aside specifically for each task. For example, Mondays could be the filming day where you do nothing but create videos. On Tuesdays, you could put aside time for nothing but editing all of the videos you made yesterday, doing keyword research on YouTube, and publishing everything. Wednesdays could be your day to snip the audio and get it ready to post on Soundcloud, iTunes and ACX, outline your writing for the next day, and get all of your keyword research done for Amazon. Thursday can be your dedicated writing day, where you transcribe your videos, clean them up for book format, and publish them to Amazon, CreateSpace and ACX. You could use Friday to chop up your book into blog posts, do some SEO research, and double check that your previous days' work has been done correctly. Saturday is when you could plan your Social Media calendar out for the week and use Hootsuite/Buffer to schedule everything to post automatically. Finally, you can take Sunday to double check your work the previous week and learn about new topics to discuss in your video the next day.

As you can see, all of this takes an enormous amount of effort and time, so planning everything out on a schedule will help you preserve some time for your social life and fun. That stuff is important too, so don't forget to let off steam every once in a while or you'll get burnt out. My second suggestion is to start off slowly. The calendar that I wrote out for you above is for an individual who is working at full capacity and focusing all efforts into building a following. You don't have to jump straight into the 24/7 grind if it isn't something that you are passionate about. Start off with one thing at a time and slowly build up. Perhaps you really enjoy making videos but nothing else. Great! Put all of your effort into building up your following on YouTube! Maybe your cup of tea is writing, so you want to focus on publishing books? Excellent! As long as you are taking action and consistently providing value to people in some way, you will find that your following will grow over time. The beauty of my system is that you can plug it into your model at any time. Have you published 40 videos already? It is never too late to snip the audio or transcribe the words. You can always repurpose content that you've already created, so if nothing else just keep pumping stuff out! You'll figure out where you want to be investing most of your efforts in time, and the pathway to your success will reveal itself.

My final suggestion is to enjoy the journey. Not every endeavor will be successful, and not every path will end up where you think it will. You may set out to accomplish one thing and stumble across an opportunity that you can't pass up. The important thing is to stay the course and keep pushing. You WILL be successful if you try hard enough for a long enough period of time and never give up. Failure is good - it is life's way of letting you know that something isn't working. Learn from your mistakes, do not dwell on them. What you will learn about the world and about yourself on this journey may be worth more to you than the original goal. And who knows, you might even have a little fun along the way.